POLAR BEARS

LIVING WILD

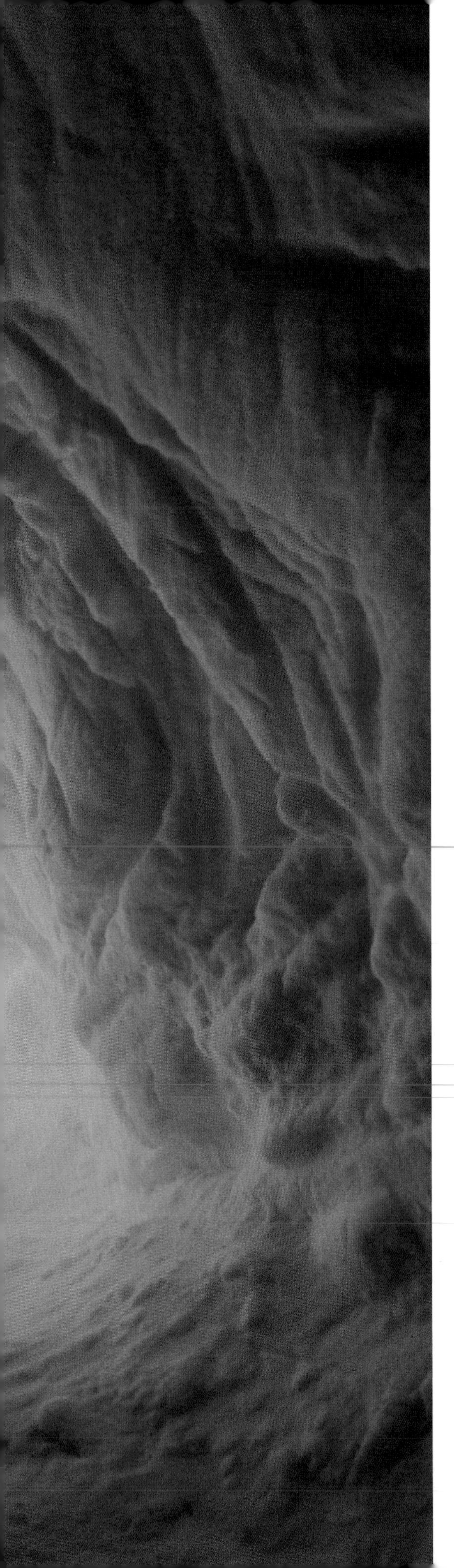

LIVING WILD

Published by Creative Education
P.O. Box 227, Mankato, Minnesota 56002
Creative Education is an imprint of The Creative Company
www.thecreativecompany.us

Design and production by Mary Herrmann
Art direction by Rita Marshall
Printed by Corporate Graphics in the United States of America

Photographs by Alamy (Arco Images GmgH, Danita Delimont, Steven J. Kazlowski), Corbis (John Conrad, Tim Davis, Stapleton Collection, Hans Strand, Kennan Ward), Getty Images (Wayne R. Bilenduke, Gary Braasch, Paul Nicklen, Pete Oxford, Norbert Rosing), iStockphoto (Michael Burton, Michel de Nijs, Dmitry Deshevykh, David T. Gomez, Christine Kilpatrick, Erlend Kvalsvik, Bev McConnell, Martina Misar, David Parsons, Thomas Pickard, John Pitcher, Richard Waghorn, Rolf Weschke, Jan Will)

Library of Congress Cataloging-in-Publication Data
Hanel, Rachael.
Polar bears / by Rachael Hanel.
p. cm. — (Living wild)
Includes bibliographical references and index.
ISBN 978-1-58341-741-6
1. Polar bear—Juvenile literature. I. Title. II. Series.

QL737.C27H364 2009
599.786—dc22 2008009502

CPSIA: 052112 PO1577
9 8 7 6 5 4

CREATIVE EDUCATION

POLAR BEARS

Rachael Hanel

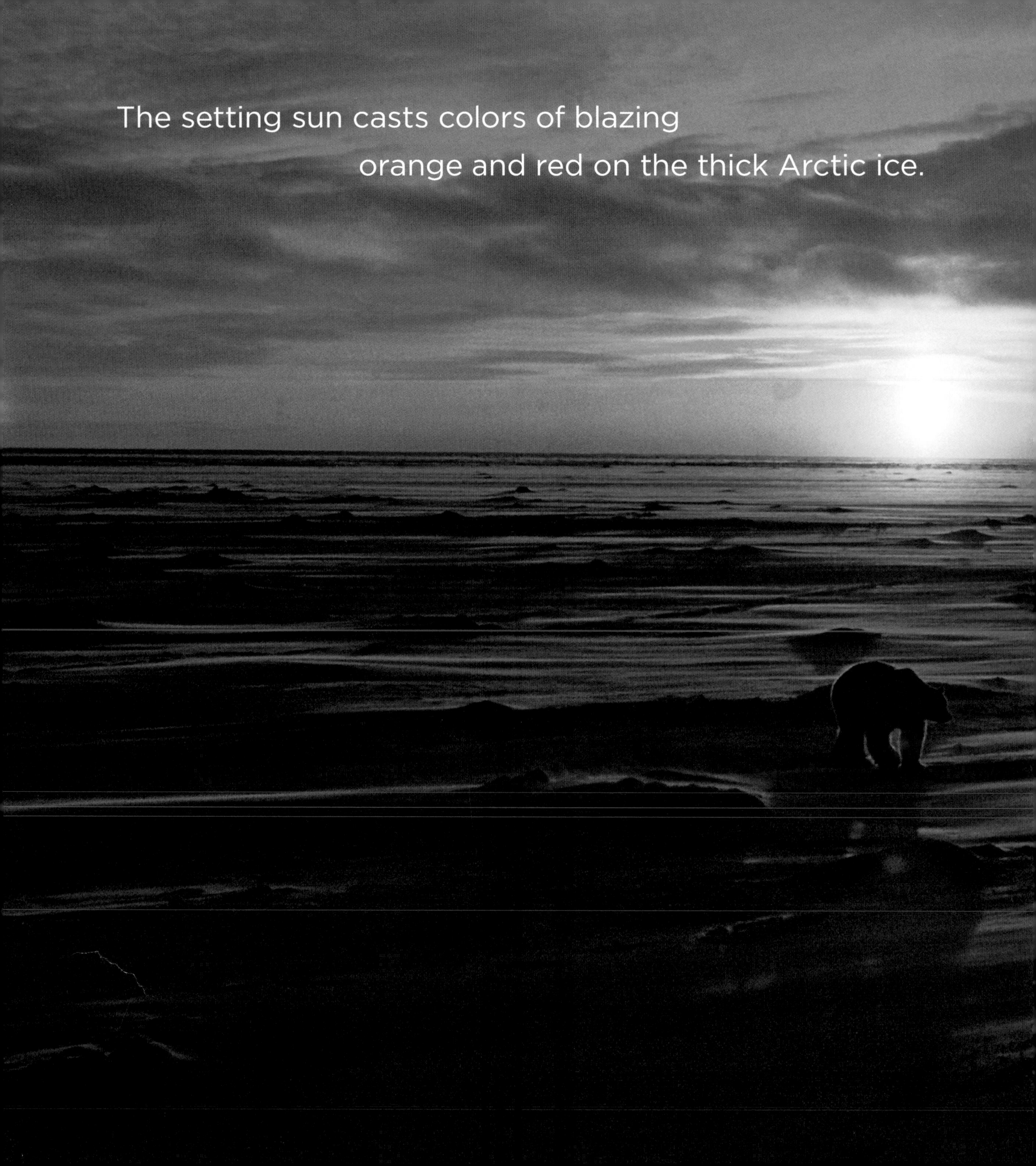

The setting sun casts colors of blazing orange and red on the thick Arctic ice.

Soon, the sun will set for several weeks,
creating a dark and frigid winter.

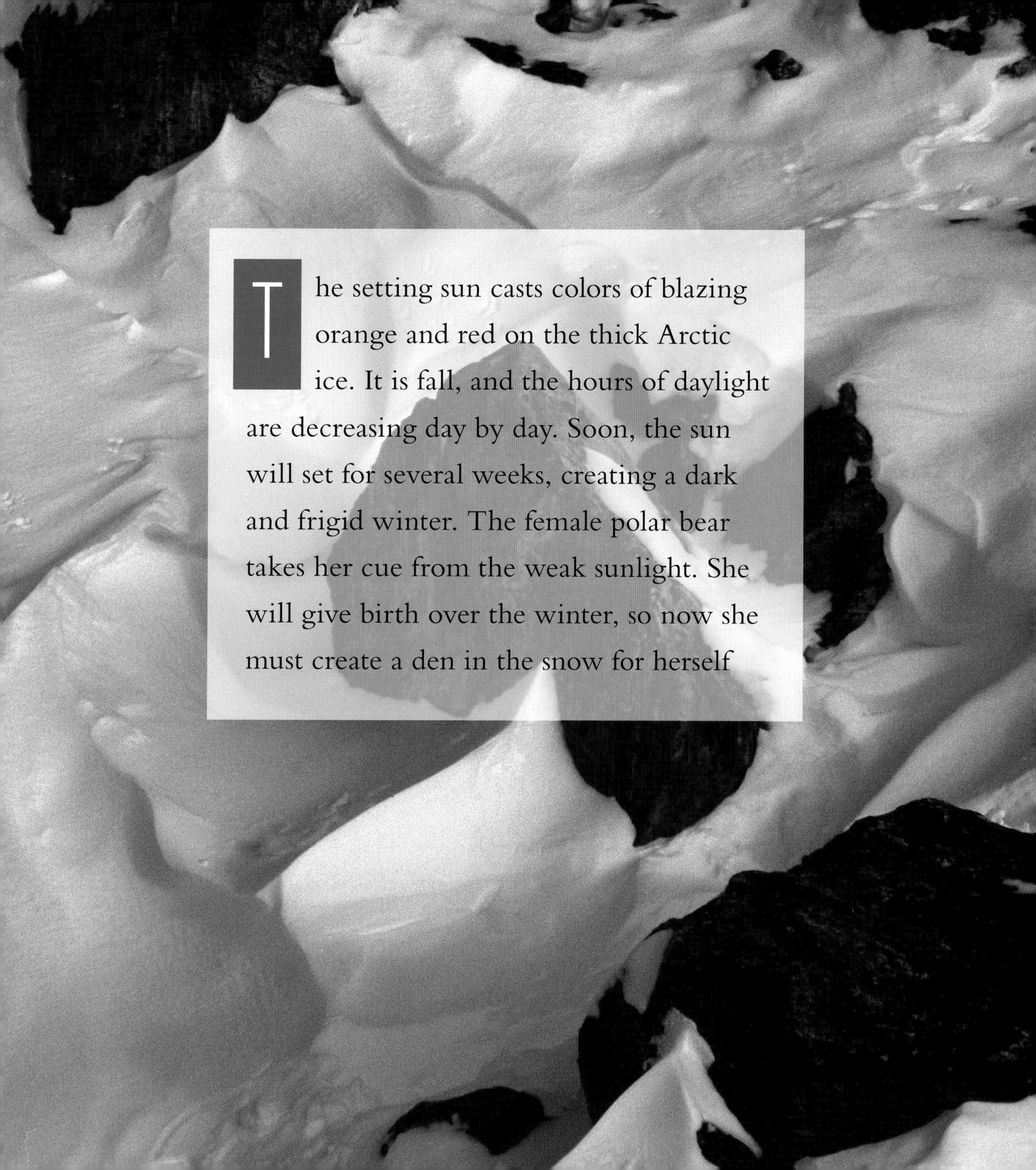

The setting sun casts colors of blazing orange and red on the thick Arctic ice. It is fall, and the hours of daylight are decreasing day by day. Soon, the sun will set for several weeks, creating a dark and frigid winter. The female polar bear takes her cue from the weak sunlight. She will give birth over the winter, so now she must create a den in the snow for herself and her cubs. She finds a deep bank of snow on a hillside. She starts digging at the snow with her massive paws, sending snow flying behind her. After a few hours, she has carved a tunnel several feet long. At one end of the tunnel, she hollows out an oval-shaped chamber. When she is finished, she is exhausted. She lies down in the chamber and falls fast asleep. She will stir in a couple of months to give birth in this cozy haven.

WHERE IN THE WORLD THEY LIVE

■ **Polar Bear**
throughout the
Arctic region

The single species of polar bear can be found in the seas and on land surrounding the Arctic Ocean, in the northernmost region of Earth known as the Arctic. Polar bears are most often found in parts of northern Alaska, Canada, Greenland, the Svalbard Islands, and Russia. The colored squares represent these northern locations.

ADAPTED TO THE COLD

The hulking polar bear is one of the largest **carnivores** in the world. It lives north of the Arctic Circle in a region called the Arctic. There, it reigns at the top of the **food chain**. The polar bear's scientific name is *Ursa maritimus*, which is Latin for "sea bear." Unlike other bears, the polar bear is considered a marine mammal. It is completely comfortable in the water. The brown bear is its closest relative.

There are an estimated 20,000 to 25,000 polar bears in the world. With its white appearance and massive bulk, there's no mistaking a polar bear for any other animal. An adult male typically weighs up to 1,700 pounds (771 kg) and can be from 8 to 10 feet (2.4–3 m) long. Adult females are much smaller, their weights usually reaching a maximum of 700 pounds (318 kg). They measure anywhere from six to eight feet (1.8–2.4 m) long.

The polar bear lives only in and around the Arctic region and can be found in parts of five countries: the United States (in Alaska only), Norway's Svalbard

The largest polar bear ever recorded was a male that weighed 2,209 pounds (1,002 kg).

Islands, Greenland (which is owned by Denmark), Russia, and Canada. It normally does not live as far north as the North Pole, as there is little food there.

Most of the time, polar bears live on large sheets of shifting ice called floes. In the winter, cooler temperatures cause the ice and the bears to move farther south. In the summer, the ice retreats, and the bears range farther north. Sometimes polar bears live on the scrubby, still-frozen land of the tundra for the summer, waiting for the ice that will take them back north.

In the winter, Arctic temperatures can plunge to -50 °F (-45 °C) or even colder for weeks on end. Every part of a polar bear's body helps it tolerate the severe cold, including its fur. Its skin is covered by two layers of fur that together measure about 1.2 to 2 inches (3–5 cm) thick. A bottom coat of thick, dense fur insulates the polar bear from extreme cold. The thinner outer layer appears white. However, the individual hairs are actually clear and hollow. Because the hollow hairs bounce

When stalking prey such as seals, a polar bear moves slowly and quietly across the ice on its broad paws.

After running or when temperatures exceed 50° F (10° C), an overheated polar bear does what it can to cool off.

back all light while absorbing none, they appear white. The light-colored fur helps the polar bear blend in with its snowy surroundings. In time, the fur can turn grimy and yellow from everyday activities such as hunting. In zoos, bears' fur can even turn green from water plants called algae that get absorbed into the hollow hair shafts. Polar bears shed their fur every spring in a process called molting. The new hair looks especially white.

A polar bear's skin is actually black, which shows through near its **muzzle** and its feet. Under the skin lies a four-inch-thick (10.2 cm) layer of blubber, or fat. The blubber, undercoat, and top coat of fur blanket the bear in warmth. In fact, despite cold temperatures, polar bears can easily overheat, especially when they run. If they overheat, they lie down and roll around on the snow or ice. A polar bear's normal body temperature is the same as a human's: 98.6 °F (37 °C).

The polar bear's massive paws help support and distribute its weight on the ice. On average, the paws measure 12 inches (30.5 cm) across. The front paws are round, while the back paws are shaped like ovals. The black pads of the paws are covered with tiny bumps

Polar bears are careful to clean themselves after a meal. They will wash in open water or use snow to scrub themselves clean.

Polar bears nap often to conserve energy, no matter where they are. Sometimes they will even use an outcropping of ice as a "pillow."

called papillae. Papillae act as rubber **nubs** that prevent a bear from slipping on the ice. Each paw has five toes, and **tufts** of fur between the toes provide further traction. A polar bear's curved claws can measure up to two inches (5 cm) long and are used to grip ice and snow. A bear walks slowly and shuffles along the ice. It might walk only two miles (3.2 km) per hour. But it can gallop if necessary, reaching speeds of up to 25 miles (40 km) per hour. However, it cannot sustain this speed for long before overheating.

The fur, blubber, and paws also play critical roles in helping a polar bear swim. The waterproof fur helps keep a bear dry and warm in the chilly water. Its thick blubber, which is less dense than seawater, keeps it afloat. And its powerful paws allow the bear to paddle with its front legs while its back legs provide direction, like the rudder on a boat. The webbed paws act as oars to effectively propel a bear through the sea. Polar bears can swim up to six miles (9.7 km) per hour and sometimes travel several miles out to sea.

The polar bear has a smaller head and longer neck than other bears. The smaller size of its head helps to minimize

A polar bear's body, with its waterproof fur and webbed paws, makes the bear well-suited to life—and play—in water.

Polar bears and glaucous gulls will both take advantage of the feasting opportunity presented by a whale carcass on the beach.

heat loss. Polar bears' ears are especially small. If the ears were any larger, it would be easy for them to freeze in cold temperatures. Its eyes are small, too, and are set deep into its head for protection from the cold and driving wind. A clear **membrane** also shields a polar bear's eyes from damaging rays known as ultraviolet light. Polar bears have sharp senses and can spot underwater prey that is as far away as 15 feet (4.6 m). Their sense of smell is especially acute, as they can smell prey from a distance of up to 20 miles (32 km).

A polar bear's 42 teeth are strong and designed to eat meat. In front, the **incisors** cut blubber and flesh from the bones of prey. Canine teeth help the bear catch fish and tear through skin. Teeth farther back in the mouth are called premolars; with these teeth, a bear grinds flesh and blubber. Teeth at the back of the mouth, called molars, are typically used to chew plants. These teeth are less well-developed in polar bears than they are in other bears that eat more plants. A polar bear generally does not chew its food thoroughly, swallowing large chunks of meat instead.

During molting, which lasts three to four months, a polar bear's dirty fur is replaced by a dazzling white coat.

Polar bears utilize blocks of floating ice to get where they want to go, leaping from one to another.

LIFE ON THE ICE

Polar bears are solitary creatures that spend most of their time resting and hunting. They are most active in the morning and early afternoon, when they search for food. A bear's preferred meal is a ringed seal. The seal lives primarily in the open water, where it feeds on shrimp and other **crustaceans**. For this reason, a polar bear will position itself on ice floes near open water. The ice floes constantly shift and move, creating rivers of open water called leads. A bear might also wait near a polynya. A polynya is an open hole of water surrounded by ice. Seals often surface at polynyas to breathe.

A polar bear might wait for hours before a seal surfaces from the water. When a seal appears, the bear grabs it with its strong forearms and drags it onto the ice. When a seal is already resting on the ice, a polar bear will lie flat on its belly and crawl toward the seal to sneak up on it. It waits until it is about 100 feet (30.5 m) away from the seal, then it charges toward the animal. In the spring, polar bears use their sense of smell to find seals and their pups in snow dens. When a bear is sure it has found a den, it rears up on its hind legs and crashes

Not all polar bears travel around the Arctic—scientists have identified 19 groups that stay in roughly the same spot.

A patient polar bear will wait by a polynya until an animal such as a seal surfaces.

When polar bears gather around a carcass, they do not fight over food. The one who made the kill usually gets to eat first.

down on the den with its front paws to break through the roof. The polar bear usually eats just the blubber and intestines of the seal. It leaves the rest of the **carcass** for **scavengers** such as the Arctic fox. A polar bear needs to eat about one 150-pound (68 kg) seal per week to survive.

Occasionally, a polar bear will feed upon hooded, harp, and bearded seals, which weigh hundreds of pounds more than the ringed seal. But these larger seals are more difficult to catch. Polar bears are also known to eat the carcasses of larger animals, such as walrus and beluga whales, that have washed up on the ice. In the summer, bears sometimes live on the tundra instead of ice. There, they feed on caribou, birds, eggs, and berries but return to the water for plants such as **kelp**.

Many polar bears travel widely throughout the year. A bear might walk 20 miles (32 km) in one day to find food. Yet populations of polar bears stay within a distinct territory, even if these territories occasionally overlap. Unlike some other animals, polar bears don't mark their territory, nor do they defend it if another group moves in. The size of a polar bear's territory depends on

Polar bears generally live and hunt by themselves, but young males are known for engaging in play-fighting.

the availability of food and the amount of ice, both of which change from year to year. A small territory may encompass 19,000 to 23,000 square miles (49,210–59,570 sq km), about the size of the state of West Virginia. A larger territory might spread over 135,000 square miles (349,648 sq km), an area slightly smaller than Montana.

Each spring, polar bears come together to mate. The female signals that she's ready to mate by a special scent that is released in her urine. The male follows the scent,

Only rarely will polar bears fight each other, and the most serious confrontations between males are over mating partners.

sometimes for several miles, until he reaches the female. If another male has arrived first, the two males may fight. They approach each other with their heads down, then rear up on their back legs to push each other. The winner of the fight mates with the female. The male bear does not help to raise the young, called cubs.

In the summer, the pregnant female eats as much as possible to store energy for her eight-month pregnancy.

As winter approaches, she burrows deep into the snow and carves out a small den, which is about six to nine feet (1.8–2.7 m) long and about six feet (1.8 m) high and wide. She will **hibernate** there until the cubs are born.

A female bear generally gives birth to two cubs, although sometimes three are born. Newborn cubs weigh only about 25 ounces (709 g) and are about 1 foot (30.5 cm) long. For several weeks, the entire family rests in the cozy den, while winds howl outside. The cubs stir only to drink their mother's nutritious milk. As the cubs grow larger, the mother carves more space out of the snowy walls of the den. She might build a short wall of snow to separate the den into two rooms.

In the spring, the mother takes her cubs outside. Each cub now weighs about 25 to 30 pounds (11.3–13.6 kg). She claws her way out of the den through several feet of snow. The cubs poke their heads out, at first blinded by the bright sun and snow. They stay close to their mother, and for the first week or two, they retreat often to the den. But gradually, the cubs spend more time outside as their thin and hungry mother searches for food after not having eaten for several months.

Bears that do not hibernate sometimes take naps out in the open.

Only pregnant polar bears hibernate. All other polar bears stay active and continue hunting throughout the winter months.

Polar bear cubs face many threats from adult males and other animals such as Arctic foxes (above). Seventy percent of cubs do not live beyond the age of three.

Once they reach a few months of age, cubs engage in play-fighting, which sharpens their hunting skills. They also communicate more vocally at this age. They whine, whimper, and growl. A mother bear will growl, hiss, or click her teeth if she or her cubs are threatened, but adult polar bears are usually quiet. For the first year, the cubs watch their mother hunt. They learn patience and hunting techniques and eat the food their mother catches. After one year, cubs will find food with their mother's help, and they will also learn to dive and swim. Cubs leave their mother after about two years. The mother is then free to mate again.

Because of their size, adult polar bears have no natural predators. Only rarely will male polar bears kill each other. However, cubs are more vulnerable. Occasionally, a male polar bear will kill cubs or a female who is protecting her cubs. An Arctic fox or wolf will attack very small cubs as well. Cubs are also more likely to die of starvation than adults because their hunting skills are less developed. Polar bears live an average of 15 to 18 years in the wild, but some have been known to reach the age of 30. In captivity, a polar bear can live about 35 years.

Since conditions are harshest in the far northern Arctic, a mother there will care for her cubs for up to three years.

Igloos, usually made of blocks of snow, were a common type of housing for the Inuits of Canada and Greenland.

BELOVED BUT THREATENED

For millennia, polar bears had no contact with humans. No man or woman dared to venture into the cold Arctic regions. But about 4,000 years ago, **Inuit** populations south of the Arctic Circle started to move farther north in search of food. When the Inuits found that they could successfully hunt in the Arctic, they soon spread out and established villages.

The Inuits respected the polar bear. They believed that the spirit of a polar bear lived on after it died. If it was treated with respect after death, its spirit would tell other polar bears to not be afraid when hunted. But if an Inuit was careless with a polar bear's remains, the people believed the bear's spirit would warn other bears. Inuit hunters used all parts of a polar bear. They ate its meat and used its skin and fur to make boots, mittens, and pants. They killed bears with spears, which required close and dangerous contact. An Inuit who killed a polar bear was honored for his bravery and courage.

The Arctic remained largely untouched by European explorers until the 1800s. Polar bears frightened early explorers, who killed as many bears as possible and sold

The earliest known captive polar bear was kept in a private zoo by Ptolemy II, who was king of Egypt from 285 to 246 B.C.

Commercial hunters have almost eliminated the polar bear from Alaska's St. Matthew Island and from coastal areas in northern Alaska.

the furs. Throughout the 1800s and into the 1900s, **commercial** hunters eliminated populations of polar bears in many parts of the Arctic. By the mid-20th century, wealthy individuals could pay a lot of money to hunt polar bears. Hunters would shoot bears from airplanes, snowmobiles, and ships. Soon, the overall polar bear population began decreasing at an alarming rate.

In 1956, due to the dwindling populations, Russia (then a state of the Soviet Union), banned polar bear hunting. In 1965, scientists from the U.S., Canada, Denmark, Norway, and the Soviet Union met in Fairbanks, Alaska, to discuss the future of the polar bear. They formed the International Union for Conservation of Nature (IUCN)/Species Survival Commission Polar Bear Specialist Group. This group shared information about the bears and coordinated research and management efforts. Those same countries signed the International Agreement on the Conservation of Polar Bears in Oslo, Norway, in 1973.

Some polar bears are still hunted today. Inuit populations in Canada are allowed to continue their ancient traditions of the polar bear hunt, even though they use rifles instead of spears. Many governments now set quotas, or limits, on the number of bears that can be killed each year to make sure the bears are not overhunted. The number of tourists who come to Canada specifically to hunt polar bears is also restricted. This type of sport hunt, led by Inuit guides, can bring in thousands of dollars for an Inuit community. Polar bear tourism is also profitable for other northern communities. Churchill, Manitoba, calls itself the "Polar Bear Capital of the World." For several weeks each year, polar bears live near this town on Canada's Hudson Bay. Tourists travel in "bear-proof" buses to see polar bears up-close.

Even though hunting no longer poses a serious threat to polar bear populations, other human activities can harm the Arctic creature. Within the past 30 years, industry has found a home in the Arctic, namely in the form of drilling for natural resources such as coal, gas, and oil. Such industrial activity increases the number of humans in the area. As more humans enter polar bear territory, the potential for disrupting the bears' habitat increases. In addition, oil drilling and shipping can result in dangerous oil spills. Oil on a bear's fur reduces its

It is not uncommon to see a polar bear walking along the streets of a city such as Churchill, Manitoba.

Even though a polar bear is suited to life in the water, many people worry that there will soon be too much water in the warming Arctic.

protection against cold and water, and a bear that ingests oil can die of poisoning.

An increasing use of chemicals and **contaminants** worldwide can affect polar bears. Ocean and air currents deposit toxins in the Arctic. The toxins gradually build up along the food chain as animals eat contaminated plants and other animals eat them. A top predator such as the polar bear then ends up ingesting a large amount of toxins from its food. While the toxins have not been shown to directly or immediately kill polar bears, scientists have noted that they can affect a bear's general health. Scientists have also found that contaminants can disrupt the bears' immune and **circulatory** systems. The long-term effects of toxins have yet to be discovered.

Because of these and other threats, the World Wildlife Fund and IUCN list the polar bear as vulnerable. This means that the animal is considered to be facing a high risk of extinction. In 2008, U.S. officials listed the bear as threatened and placed it under the protection of the Endangered Species Act.

Polar bears have always captured the imagination of humans. The polar bear's entry into worldwide zoos in the early 20th century gave more people access to this exotic creature. The most famous zoo polar bear is undoubtedly Knut. Knut and his brother were born in late 2006 in Germany's Berlin Zoo. For an unknown reason, their mother rejected the cubs and refused to feed them. Knut's brother died after only four days. But a zookeeper cared for Knut around the clock for several months, even sleeping on a mattress next to the cub, until the cub began to thrive. Some animal rights activists argued that the

Captive polar bears are given toys with which to play and are kept in secure, controlled environments.

zookeeper was wrong to have fed Knut and that nature should have been allowed to take its course. The effort to save Knut attracted worldwide attention. He earned the rhyming nickname "Cute Knut" and was often photographed. The Berlin Zoo made millions of dollars through ticket sales and through the licensing of Knut's image for toys, books, and clothes.

Polar bears are associated with the icy North. For this reason, they have turned up in advertisements for heating and cooling systems, ice cream, and beverages. In

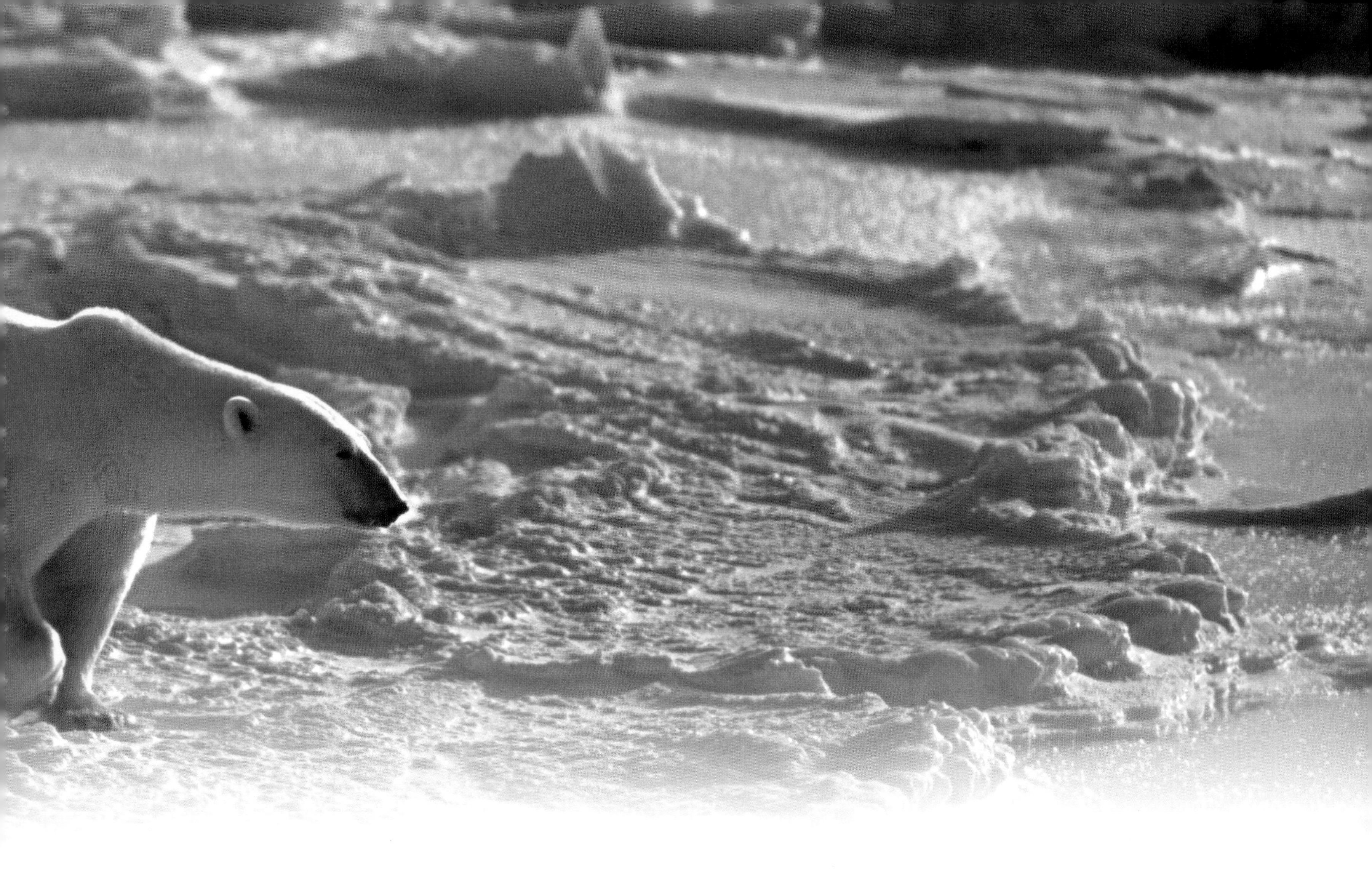

ads, they have often been pictured with penguins, even though the two animals live on opposite ends of Earth. Coca-Cola adopted the polar bear in its advertising in 1993. The first television ad to feature the bears showed them in the Arctic, sipping Coca-Colas while watching a dazzling display of northern lights in the sky. The polar bear commercials were especially popular during the winter holidays. In 2008, Coca-Cola partnered with the World Wildlife Fund to help reduce the causes of global warming and protect polar bears' environments.

Without the ice that covers so much Arctic water during the winter, polar bears would have difficulty traveling.

A WARMING ENVIRONMENT

Scientists think that polar bears are a relatively new species in terms of **evolution**. For decades, polar bears were thought to have appeared about 100,000 years ago. But a new fossil found in 2007 may be 110,000 to 130,000 years old. A major warming period occurred more than 100,000 years ago, and if the bears had indeed been alive before that time, then they somehow survived the change in temperatures. This discovery of such an adaptation could bode well for the polar bear's uncertain future.

Polar bears are believed to be descendants of the brown bear. One theory proposes that a group of brown bears traveled far north and were trapped by glaciers thousands of years ago. They then adapted to the icy environment. Even though polar bears and brown bears are closely related, the polar bear has undergone numerous changes to adapt to life in the Arctic. For example, a female polar bear produces milk that is composed of 33 percent fat, as opposed to between 20 and 25 percent in brown bears. The rich milk of a polar bear provides the extra energy cubs need to grow strong in a cold climate.

The brown bear (above) is much more accustomed to feeding on fish than is its relative the polar bear (opposite).

When the sea ice breaks up, it is time for a polar bear to return to land, where its food choices will be more limited.

Scientific observation of polar bears first began in the early 20th century, but it wasn't until the 1960s that serious research on polar bear populations started. Today, polar bears are monitored through collars that use **satellites** to track their movements. Only females can wear collars. Males have wider necks and narrower heads than females, so collars placed on them can easily fall off. Tracking can also protect polar bears. For example, the winter dens of female polar bears are not visible to the naked eye, which makes them vulnerable to human disturbance. Monitoring the bears allows scientists to keep track of occupied dens, and they can alert other people to the dens' presence. Monitoring also helps scientists keep a more accurate tally of population counts. This enables governments to determine the number of hunting permits to allow in certain regions.

Other studies try to predict what the future will look like for polar bears, as knowing how they might fare in the future can help people create methods to protect them now. The U.S. Geological Survey (USGS), along with other governmental agencies, recently researched the bears' status. In two regions of the Arctic, the study found, polar bear numbers are expected to drop dramatically by the year 2060. In other areas, a decline was also predicted in 75 to 100 years. Disturbingly, the USGS indicated that Alaska's polar bear population is expected to disappear altogether by the year 2050. All of these projected population declines will likely be due to the decreased availability of sea ice as a result of warmer temperatures in the Arctic.

The most extensive studies related to polar bears concern the effects of the gradual increase in Earth's temperature, an event known as global warming. The Arctic, with its vast regions of ice, shows visible signs of global warming earlier than the rest of the planet. As the Arctic's most well-known creatures, polar bears can serve as a key indicator of the entire planet's health.

Evidence that the Arctic is warming has been mounting for decades. Western Hudson Bay researchers have been tracking the polar bear since 1981. Since that time, they have observed an earlier seasonal breakup of sea ice. In recent years, researchers have found that the ice is melting earlier in the summer and freezing later in the winter than ever before. Polar bears need sea ice from

A mother bear might return to the same den year after year. Sometimes, several females will hibernate close to each other.

Sometimes, the ice melts so quickly that a bear can find itself on a solitary ice pack far out to sea.

which to hunt seals. A shorter ice season means less time to hunt. This causes a major disruption in polar bears' feeding habits. As a result, many polar bears now weigh less and give birth to fewer cubs.

When the sea ice breaks up earlier than normal and polar bears are forced onto land earlier in the year due to lack of sea ice, they may not have enough blubber reserves to last until the ice appears again. Female bears stranded on land also cannot return to their dens to hibernate. They are forced to find new, less desirable dens, and this may put their cubs at risk.

Global warming is leading to larger numbers of polar bears living near Churchill, Manitoba. This increases the number of tourists eager to see the bears. But the human-bear interaction can often result in trouble. Hungry bears creep into town and forage through garbage cans. At one time, humans would have shot and killed such bears. But now, people are encouraged to call wildlife patrol officers, who scare off the bears using non-lethal means. Stubborn bears are tranquilized and transported north by helicopter.

Unfortunately, polar bears do not rebound quickly from severe population declines because a mother gives

As long as icebergs abound in the Arctic waters of northern Canada, polar bears can rest and hunt easily.

A popular theory about how a polar bear's hollow hair shafts conduct light to its black skin, thus keeping it warm, was disproved in 1988.

birth to only a couple of cubs at a time, and litters are often years apart. This makes the bears even more vulnerable to the effects of global warming and human interference. But for the past several years, polar bear populations have remained steady. Thanks to measures taken to stop and steeply reduce hunting, they have recovered from 19th- and 20th-century overhunting, which has been the single biggest threat posed to their survival thus far.

Unlike many other threatened species, polar bears have been able to continue living in their natural habitat. Although they face some human interference, the cold Arctic keeps most humans away. People, for the most part, do not **encroach** upon polar bears' territory in large numbers.

Polar bears have always held special meaning to humans, from the Inuit of hundreds of years ago to fans of baby Knut today. Humans will not let polar bears disappear without a fight. Scientists and researchers are keeping a close eye on the great bears, and advancements in technology, such as satellites, make it easier than ever to track them. As numerous government agencies and

private foundations continue to fight the effects of global warming, they hope to lessen the threats facing polar bears and make the world a safer place.

Scientists representing different countries often work together on projects to monitor polar bear populations.

ANIMAL TALE: THE OLD WOMAN AND THE POLAR BEAR CUB

The Inuit are known for their strong oral traditions. For generations, they have spent many cold winter nights indoors, telling stories by the fire all night long. One popular story that has endured through the years involves an old woman and a polar bear cub. It is a tale of friendship, heartbreak, and the courage to do what is right.

Long ago, there lived an old woman in an Inuit village. She lived by herself. Other people in the village shared food with her that they had caught while hunting. One day, another woman appeared at her window.

"Would you like a polar bear cub?" the woman asked her. "The men of the village killed a mother polar bear, and now her cub is left behind."

The old woman nodded. "Oh yes, I would like the company," she said. "I will take the cub."

The old woman fed the cub the blubber of seals. He slept with her at night. She talked to him, and he started to think like a human.

The cub grew big and strong. In the summers, he left the house and hunted in the water. In the winter, he hunted on the ice. He always brought back plenty of food for the old woman. She no longer had to rely on the men of the village to bring her food.

The village children delighted in playing with the bear. The bear was always careful to cover his claws when he played with the children, so as not to hurt them.

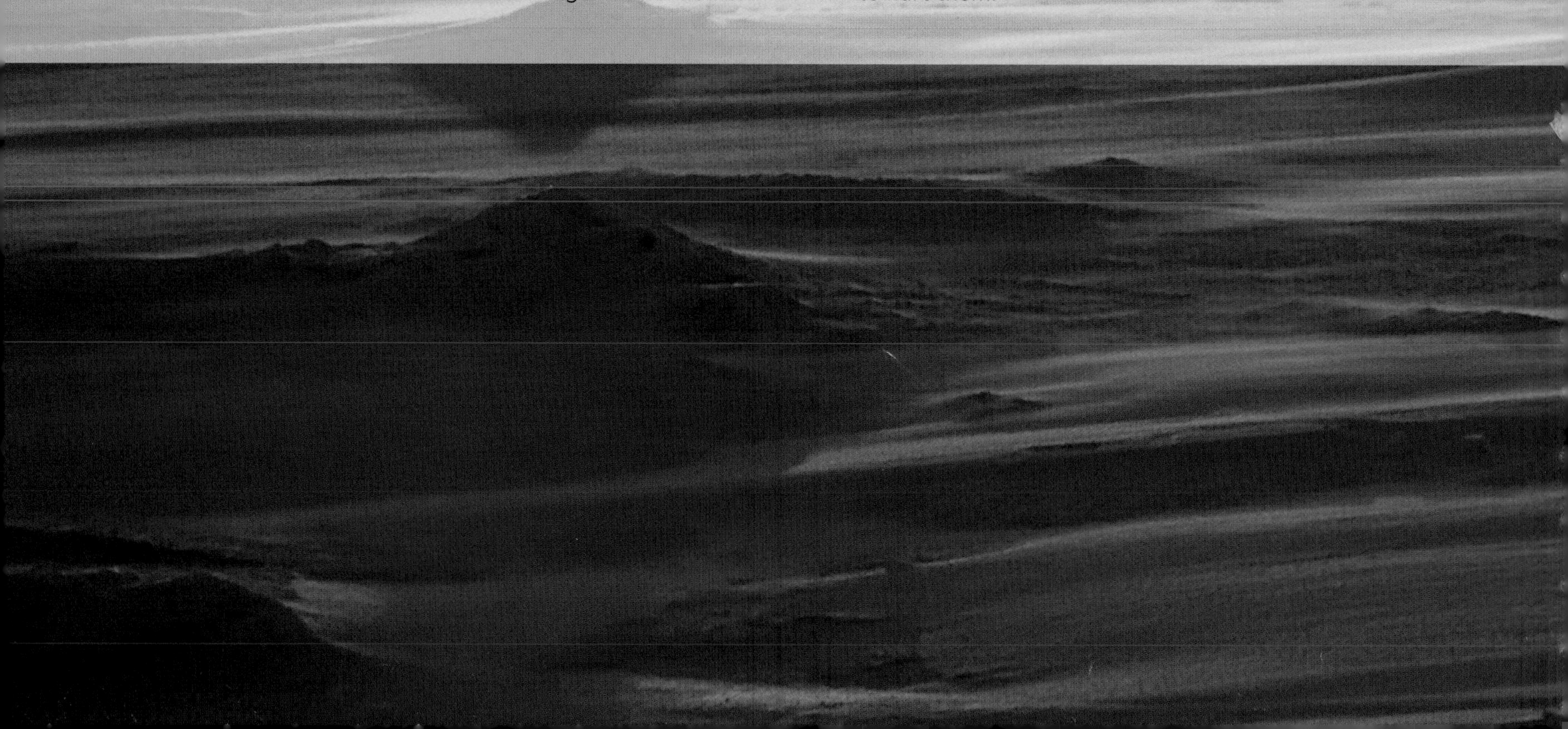

Sometimes, the men of the village would take the bear hunting with them. The bear always caught a lot of food, but the men were not as lucky. The men started to get jealous because the bear was a better hunter than they were. They decided they would kill him.

But some children overheard the men's plan, and they ran to the old woman's house, shouting, "Old woman! We heard the men say they want to kill the bear. Oh please, do not let anything happen to him!"

The old woman became sick with worry. What would she do without her companion? She needed to keep him safe. She lay awake at night, wondering what to do. Finally, she made a decision and spoke to the bear.

"Dear friend," said the old woman, "I am afraid you are in danger if you stay here with me. It is time that you go live with your own kind. Please, in the morning, you must go."

At daybreak, the old woman stood in her doorway with the bear. Tears streamed down her face. Before the bear left, she dipped her hands in oil. As she hugged the bear, she took one hand and left a long, black streak on his side.

The polar bear left, and the old woman was alone once again. But on clear days, she would walk far from the village. Sometimes, she spotted a polar bear with a black mark on its side. To this day, some Inuit believe a large bear with a black streak still wanders the icy plains of the Arctic.

GLOSSARY

carcass - the dead body of an animal

carnivores - animals that feed upon the meat of other animals

circulatory - relating to the movement of blood through the body

commercial - used for business and to gain a profit rather than for personal reasons

contaminants - non-natural substances that have a negative effect upon the environment and animals

crustaceans - water creatures such as shrimp, lobsters, and crabs, which have a hard outer shell

encroach - to intrude gradually into the space of another; going beyond prescribed boundaries

evolution - the process of adapting to survive in a certain environment

food chain - a system in nature in which living things are dependent on each other for food

hibernate - to spend the winter in a sleep-like state in which breathing and heart rate slow down

incisors - the front teeth that are used to cut through food

Inuit - people native to northern Canada and parts of Alaska and Greenland, sometimes called Eskimo

kelp - a type of seaweed found in ocean waters

membrane - a thin, clear layer of tissue that covers an internal organ or developing limb

muzzle - the part of an animal's head that includes the jaws and nose

nubs - small lumps that stick out from the surface of an object

satellites - mechanical devices launched into space; they may be designed to travel around Earth or toward other planets or the sun

scavengers - animals that eat the rotting flesh of dead animals

tufts - extensions of feathers or hair that usually form a ridge or fluffy ball

SELECTED BIBLIOGRAPHY

Banks, Martin. *The Polar Bear on the Ice*. Milwaukee: Gareth Stevens Publishing, 1989.

Dabcovich, Lydia. *The Polar Bear Son*. New York: Clarion Books, 1997.

DuTemple, Lesley. *Polar Bears*. Minneapolis: Lerner Publishing, 1997.

Matthews, Downs. *Polar Bear Cubs*. New York: Simon & Schuster, 1989.

Polar Bears International. "Homepage." Polar Bears International. http://www.polarbearsinternational.org/.

Seaworld. "Polar Bears." Seaworld. http://www.seaworld.org/infobooks/PolarBears/home.html.

The Arctic sea ice on which polar bears live gets thicker when floes bump into each other, creating ridges.

INDEX

activities 15, 16, 21, 22, 25–26, 39, 40
- caring for cubs 25–26
- hibernation 25, 39, 40
- hunting 15, 21, 25, 40
- resting 16, 21, 25
- swimming 16, 26
- traveling 16, 21, 22

conservation measures 30, 33, 38–40, 42, 43
- Endangered Species Act 33
- international agreements 30
- research 30, 38–40

cubs 8, 24, 25–26, 33, 37, 40, 42, 44
- appearance at birth 25
- learning skills 26
- litters of 25, 42
- need for mother's milk 25, 37
- vulnerability of 26

cultural influences 29, 30–31, 34–35, 40, 42, 44
- advertising 34–35
- on Inuit peoples 29, 30–31, 42, 44
- tourism 31, 40

dens 7–8, 25, 38, 39, 40

evolution 37

food chains 11, 32

habitats 7, 11, 12, 21, 22–23, 29, 30, 31, 39, 40, 42
- Alaska 11, 30, 39
- Arctic Circle 11, 29
- Canada 12, 30, 31
- Greenland 12
- Hudson Bay 31, 39
- ice 7, 12, 21, 22, 39, 40
- Russia 12, 30
- Svalbard Islands 11
- territory size 22–23
- tundra 12, 22

life expectancy 26

mating 23–24, 26

physical characteristics 8, 11, 12, 15–16, 19, 22, 26, 29, 30, 31, 38, 40, 42
- blubber 15, 16, 40
- coloring 12, 15
- eyes 19
- fur 12, 15, 16, 29, 30, 31
- paws 8, 15–16, 22
- sizes 11
- skin 12, 15, 29, 42
- small head 16, 19, 38
- teeth 19, 26

populations 11, 22, 30, 31, 38, 39, 40, 42

predators 26

prey 19, 21–22, 40
- birds 22
- carcasses 22
- caribou 22
- eggs 22
- seals 21–22, 40

relationship with humans 29, 42

relatives 11, 37
- ancestors 37
- brown bears 11, 37

scientific monitoring 38, 42

scientific name 11

senses 19, 21

social behaviors 24, 26
- communication 26
- domination for mate 24

speeds 16

threatened status 33, 42

threats 26, 29, 30–33, 35, 38, 39, 40, 42, 43
- climate change *see* global warming
- contaminants 32–33
- global warming 39, 40, 42, 43
- hunting by humans 29, 30–31, 38, 42
- industrial activities 31–32
- starvation 26

zoos 15, 29, 33–34, 42
- and popularity of Knut 33–34, 42